POEMS *to* PERFORM

For my sister Mary

First published 2013 by Macmillan Children's Books
A division of Macmillan Publishers Limited
20 New Wharf Road, London N1 9RR
Basingstoke and Oxford
www.panmacmillan.com

Associated companies throughout the world

ISBN: 978-0-230-75743-1

2 4 6 8 9 7 5 3 1

A CIP catalogue record for this book is available from the British Library.

Printed and bound by CPI Group (UK) Ltd, Croydon CR0 4YY

JULIA DONALDSON

POEMS to PERFORM

MACMILLAN CHILDREN'S BOOKS

Contents

Foreword

There are already a number of excellent books of poems which are good to read aloud, but this one is a little different. All the poems in it lend themselves to being recited by more than one voice.

Like most children, I always loved acting, and when I received a poetry anthology for my fifth birthday I soon memorised many of the poems and taught them to my younger sister Mary. We used to enjoy declaiming the ones in which we could each take a part, like Rose Fyleman's poem, "Conversation", about Mousie, Mousie in which someone (a cat, I think) is trying to lure a wary mouse out of its hiding-place.

When you think about it, role-play is something entirely natural, starting with dolls, teddies and farmyard animals, and carrying on into playground games. But I can't help feeling that children sometimes have their love of drama and performance squashed out of them; it tends to be regarded as a form of showing off and therefore to be frowned on. This is a shame, because in my opinion performance is such a good way of increasing self-confidence.

When I became the Children's Laureate in 2011 I knew I wanted to help teachers and their classes – and families, too – do more performing. So I've written some plays and created a website about classroom drama, and I've also been collecting the poems for this anthology. Some of these were old favourites, like Edward Lear's "The Jumblies" which my grandmother used to recite to me. Others, such as Michael Rosen's

"The Rhythm of Life", were exciting discoveries, and yet others, including Clare Bevan's thought-provoking "The Treasures", have been specially commissioned. There is even one poem by a child, Ciarán Powders, who wrote "London 2012" for a competition about the Olympic Games.

Here you will find poems for just two voices, poems for groups to recite, and poems which can be performed by a whole class. Many of them are conversations, between characters as diverse as a teacher and pupil, a goblin and a nymph, and a tree and a pool. There is even one dialogue between two ends of the same worm! I couldn't resist including "Soldier, Soldier, Won't You Marry Me?", perhaps because it brings back a memory of losing my first tooth. (Our class used to perform this poem with all the girls marching forward in a row to woo the soldier; I marched so enthusiastically that I banged into the opposite wall.)

Then there are poems where the chorus can be recited by a whole class while the verses are divided up between different voices. There are chants, tongue-twisters, poems with sound effects, and others, such as my own "Nut Tree", which lend themselves to actions. Or you might think about performing some of the poems in sign language as well as vocally.

I hope there will be something here for everyone. The themes include school, animals, football, dinosaurs and magic, and the moods range from funny to serious to scary. While some of the poems are quite young and simple, others, such as W. H. Auden's "O What is That Sound", a chilling drama of betrayal, are more challenging.

If you enjoy the poems, I hope you may want to perform them to an audience. You could either select a few poems for small groups, or a couple of longer ones for a whole class. You could even think about simple props and costumes for some of the poems, such as James Carter's "Pirate Pete" or the traditional "The Wraggle Taggle Gipsies". At the back of the book there are suggestions for performing each poem, but there is no need to feel bound by these.

I thought hard about what sort of illustrations the poems should have: without any, many children might wonder, like Alice, "What's a book without any pictures?", and yet I was wary of limiting the reader's imaginative response to each poem. When I discovered Clare Melinsky's work I knew she was The One, and I am absolutely delighted with her sensitive and characterful linocuts.

I hope that you will agree that Clare's illustrations make this not just a useful but a beautiful book, one which will appeal to any reader. Although it is called *Poems to Perform* there is nothing to stop you reading the poems silently to yourself. After all, the performance can always go on in your head.

Julia Donaldson, March 2013

The Rhythm of Life

Hand on the bridge
feel the rhythm of the train.

Hand on the window
feel the rhythm of the rain.

Hand on your throat
feel the rhythm of your talk.

Hand on your leg
feel the rhythm of your walk.

Hand in the sea
feel the rhythm of the tide.

Hand on your heart
feel the rhythm inside.

Hand on the rhythm
feel the rhythm of the rhyme.

Hand on your life
feel the rhythm of time
Hand on your life
feel the rhythm of time
Hand on your life
feel the rhythm of time.

MICHAEL ROSEN

Voices of Water

The water in the rain says
                    Tick Tick Tack
The water in the sleet says
                    Slush
The water in the ice says
                    Crick Crick Crack
The water in the snow says
                    Hush

The water in the sink says
                    Slosh Slosh
The water in the tap says
                    Drip
The water in the bath says
                    Wash Wash
The water in the cup says
                    Sip

The water in the pool says

> *Splish Splash*

The water in the stream says

> *Trill*

The water in the sea says

> *Crish Crash*

The water in the pond . . .

> stays still.

The water in the soil says

> *Sow, Sow*

The water in the cloud says

> *Give*

The water in the plant says

> *Grow, Grow*

The water in the world says

> *Live*

TONY MITTON

The Sound Collector

A stranger called this morning
Dressed all in black and grey
Put every sound into a bag
And carried them away.

The whistling of the kettle
The turning of the lock
The purring of the kitten
The ticking of the clock

The popping of the toaster
The crunching of the flakes
When you spread the marmalade
The scraping sound it makes

The hissing of the frying-pan
The ticking of the grill
The bubbling of the bathtub
As it starts to fill

The drumming of the raindrops
On the window-pane
When you do the washing-up
The gurgle of the drain

The crying of the baby
The squeaking of the chair
The swishing of the curtain
The creaking of the stair

A stranger called this morning
He didn't leave his name
Left us only silence
Life will never be the same.

ROGER McGOUGH

You Can't Stop Me!

High up in the heather
where nobody was,
and no noise was, but birdsong,
and nothing moved, but the breeze,
something began.

First a ripple
then a gurgle
and a small snake of water
spilled its way downhill.
"You can't stop me,"
Burbled the little brook,
"Not now, not ever . . . never."
And it chattered its way
over pebbles
down waterfalls
past cows
into a splashing stream . . .

"You can't stop me,"
Sang the stream,
"Not now, not ever . . . never."
It swished
it swirled
through willows
round fishermen
past swans
into a rolling river.
"YOU CAN'T STOP ME,"
chanted the rolling river . . .
"NOT NOW, NOT EVER . . . NEVER!"
It flounced
It flowed
under bridges
round barges
past smokestacks
into a swollen river . . .

"YOU CAN'T STOP ME,"
swelled the swollen river . . .
"NOT NOW, NOT EVER . . . NEVER!"
It bulged
it slid
past workers
under gulls
to bobbing boats
and the swaying sea . . .

"YOU CAN'T STOP ME,"
Roared the mighty river.
"NOT NOW, NOT EVER . . . NEVER!"

"Oh Hush," said the sea,
as it swallowed it up.

MIRIAM MOSS

The Jumblies

They went to sea in a Sieve, they did,
    In a Sieve they went to sea:
In spite of all their friends could say,
On a winter's morn, on a stormy day,
    In a Sieve they went to sea!
And when the Sieve turned round and round,
And every one cried, "You'll all be drowned!"
They called aloud, "Our Sieve ain't big,
But we don't care a button! we don't care a fig!
    In a Sieve we'll go to sea!"
      Far and few, far and few,
        Are the lands where the Jumblies live;
        Their heads are green, and their hands are blue,
        And they went to sea in a Sieve.

They sailed away in a Sieve, they did,
    In a Sieve they sailed so fast,
With only a beautiful pea-green veil
Tied with a riband by way of a sail,
    To a small tobacco-pipe mast;
And every one said, who saw them go,
"O won't they be soon upset, you know!
For the sky is dark, and the voyage is long,

And happen what may, it's extremely wrong
    In a Sieve to sail so fast!"
        Far and few, far and few,
            Are the lands where the Jumblies live;
        Their heads are green, and their hands are blue,
            And they went to sea in a Sieve.

The water it soon came in, it did,
    The water it soon came in;
So to keep them dry, they wrapped their feet
In a pinky paper all folded neat,
    And they fastened it down with a pin.
And they passed the night in a crockery-jar,
And each of them said, "How wise we are!
Though the sky be dark, and the voyage be long,
Yet we never can think we were rash or wrong,
    While round in our Sieve we spin!"
        Far and few, far and few,
            Are the lands where the Jumblies live;
        Their heads are green, and their hands are blue,
            And they went to sea in a Sieve.

And all night long they sailed away;
    And when the sun went down,
They whistled and warbled a moony song
To the echoing sound of a coppery gong,
    In the shade of the mountains brown.
"O Timballo! How happy we are,
When we live in a Sieve and a crockery-jar.
And all night long in a the moonlight pale,
We sail away with a pea-green sail,
    In the shade of the mountains brown!"
        Far and few, far and few,
            Are the lands where the Jumblies live;
            Their heads are green, and their hands are blue,
            And they went to sea in a Sieve.

They sailed to the Western Sea, they did,
    To a land all covered with trees,
And they bought an Owl, and a useful Cart,
And a pound of Rice, and a Cranberry Tart,
    And a hive of silvery Bees.
And they bought a Pig, and some green Jack-daws,
And a lovely Monkey with lollipop paws,
And forty bottles of Ring-Bo-Ree,
    And no end of Stilton Cheese.

Far and few, far and few,
    Are the lands where the Jumblies live;
Their heads are green, and their hands are blue,
    And they went to sea in a Sieve.

And in twenty years they all came back,
    In twenty years or more,
And every one said, "How tall they've grown!
For they've been to the Lakes, and the Torrible Zone,
    And the hills of the Chankly Bore;"
And they drank their health, and gave them a feast
Of dumplings made of beautiful yeast;
And every one said, "If we only live,
We too will go to sea in a Sieve,—
    To the hills of the Chankly Bore!"
        Far and few, far and few,
            Are the lands where the Jumblies live;
        Their heads are green, and their hands are blue,
            And they went to sea in a Sieve.

EDWARD LEAR

The Tree and the Pool

"I don't want my leaves to drop," said the tree.
"I don't want to freeze," said the pool.
"I don't want to smile," said the sombre man,
"Or ever to cry," said the Fool.

"I don't want to open," said the bud,
"I don't want to end," said the night.
"I don't want to rise," said the neap-tide,
"Or ever to fall," said the kite.

They wished and they murmured and whispered,
They said that to change was a crime.
Then a voice from nowhere answered,
"You must do what I say," said Time.

BRIAN PATTEN

Nut Tree

Small, brown, hard, round,
The nut is lying underground.
Now a shoot begins to show.
Now the shoot begins to grow,
Tall, taller, tall as can be.
The shoot is growing into a tree,
And branches grow and stretch and spread
With twigs and leaves above your head.
And on a windy autumn day
The nut tree bends, the branches sway,
The leaves fly off and whirl around,
And nuts go tumbling to the ground,
Small, brown, hard, round.

JULIA DONALDSON

My Colours

These are
My colours,
One by one:

Red –
The poppies
Where I run.

Orange –
Summer's
Setting sun.

Yellow –
Farmers'
Fields of corn.

Green –
The clover
On my lawn.

Blue –
The sea
Where fishes spawn.

Indigo –
A starling's
Feather.

Violet –
The dancing
Heather.

A rainbow
They make
All together.

COLIN WEST

Twenty-Four Hours

Twenty-four hours
  Make a night and a day;
Never a minute more
  Will one stay.

One o'clock sounds
  To the owl's cold cry;
Two, as the flame of the fox
  Glimmers by.

Three, the still hour
  Of the moon and the star;
Four, the first cock-crow
  Is heard from afar.

Five, and the bird-song
  Already begun;
Six, the bright mail van
  Comes up with the sun.

Seven, here's the milk
    With the butter and cream;
Eight, all the kettles
    Are letting off steam.

Nine, the school bell
    Calls the lazy and late;
Ten, as the children
    Chant, "Two fours are eight."

Eleven, and it's cooking
    With pot, pan and spoon;
Twelve, and the morning
    Says, "Good afternoon!"

One, and for dinner
    Hot pudding and pie;
Two, all the dishes
    Are watered and dry.

Three, the quick water-hen
    Hides in the pool;
Four, as the children
    Come smiling from school.

Five, see the milking cows
    Lurch down the lane;
Six, and the family
    Together again.

Seven, and the children
    Are bathed and in bed;
Eight, dad is snoozing,
    The paper unread.

Nine, and the house mouse
    Squints out of his hole;
Ten, and the tabby cat
    Takes a dark stroll.

Eleven, bolt the window
   And lock the front door;
Twelve o'clock strikes
   And on sea and on shore
Night and day's journey
   Is starting once more.
Twelve o'clock sounds
   On the steep and the plain,
Day and night's journey
   Beginning again.

CHARLES CAUSLEY

My True Love

On Monday, Monday,
My true love said to me
I've brought you this nice pumpkin
I picked it off a tree!

On Tuesday, Tuesday,
My true love said to me
"Look – I've brought you sand tarts
I got them by the sea.

On Wednesday, Wednesday,
My true love said to me
I've caught you this white polar bear
It came from Tennessee

On Thursday, Thursday
My true love said to me
This singing yellow butterfly
I've all for you, from me.

On Friday, Friday
My true love said to me
Here's a long-tailed guinea pig
It's frisky as can be.

On Saturday, Saturday
To my true love I said
You have not told me ONE
    TRUE THING,
So you I'll never wed!

ANON

Soldier, Soldier, Won't You Marry Me?

O soldier, soldier, won't you marry me
With your musket fife and drum?
O no sweet maid I cannot marry you
For I have no coat to put on.

So up she went to her grandfather's chest
And she got him a coat of the very, very best,
She got him a coat of the very, very best,
And the soldier put it on.

O soldier, soldier, won't you marry me
With your musket fife and drum?
O no sweet maid I cannot marry you,
For I have no hat to put on.

So up she went to her grandfather's chest
And she got him a hat of the very, very best,
She got him a hat of the very, very best,
And the soldier put it on.

O soldier, soldier, won't you marry me
With your musket fife and drum?
O no sweet maid I cannot marry you
For I have no gloves to put on.

So up she went to her grandfather's chest
And she got him a pair of the very, very best,
She got him a pair of the very, very best
And the soldier put them on.

O soldier, soldier, won't you marry me
With your musket fife and drum?
O no sweet maid I cannot marry you
For I have no boots to put on.

So up she went to her grandfather's chest
And she got him a pair of the very, very best,
She got him a pair of the very, very best,
And the soldier put them on.

O soldier, soldier, won't you marry me
With your musket fife and drum?
O no sweet maid I cannot marry you
For I have for I have a wife of my own.

ANON

Caribbean Counting Poem

One by one
one by one
waves are dancing in the sun.

Two by two
two by two
seashells pink
and purply-blue.

Three by three
three by three
big boats
putting out to sea.

Four by four
four by four
children fishing
on the shore.

Five by five
five by five
little walking
fish arrive.

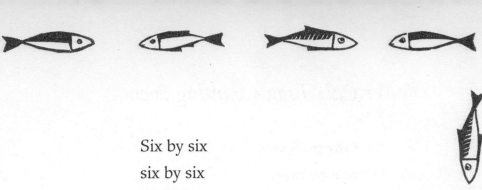

Six by six
six by six
pelicans
performing tricks.

Seven by seven
seven by seven
puffy clouds
patrolling heaven.

Eight by eight
eight by eight
fishes nibbling
juicy bait.

Nine by nine
nine by nine
taking home
a catch that's fine.

Ten by ten
ten by ten
tomorrow we
will come again.

PAMELA MORDECAI

The Wraggle Taggle Gipsies

There were three gipsies a-come to my door,
    And down-stairs ran this lady, O!
One sang high, and another sang low,
    And the other sang, Bonny, bonny, Biscay, O!

Then she pulled off her silk finished gown
    And put on hose of leather, O!
The ragged, ragged rags about our door—
    She's gone with the wraggle taggle gipsies, O!

It was late last night, when my lord came home,
    Enquiring for his a-lady, O!
The servants said on every hand:
    "She's gone with the wraggle taggle gipsies, O!"

"O saddle to me my milk-white steed,
    Go and fetch me my pony, O!
That I may ride and seek my bride,
    Who is gone with the wraggle taggle gipsies, O!"

O he rode high and he rode low,
    He rode through woods and copses too,
Until he came to an open field,
    And there he espied his a-lady, O!

"What makes you leave your house and land?
    What makes you leave your money, O?
What makes you leave your new-wedded lord;
    To go with the wraggle taggle gipsies, O?"

"What care I for my house and my land?
    What care I for my money, O?
What care I for my new-wedded lord?
    I'm off with the wraggle taggle gipsies, O!"

"Last night you slept on a goose-feather bed,
    With the sheet turned down so bravely, O!
And to-night you'll sleep in a cold open field,
    Along with the wraggle taggle gipsies, O!"

"What care I for a goose-feather bed,
    With the sheet turned down so bravely, O!
For to-night I shall sleep in a cold open field,
    Along with the wraggle taggle gipsies, O!"

ANON

Spells

I dance and dance without any feet –
This is the spell of the ripening wheat.

With never a tongue I've a tale to tell –
This is the meadow-grasses' spell.

I give you health without any fee –
This is the spell of the apple-tree.

I rhyme and riddle without any book –
This is the spell of the bubbling brook.

Without any legs I run for ever –
This is the spell of the mighty river.

I fall for ever and not at all –
This is the spell of the waterfall.

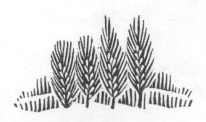

Without a voice I roar aloud –
This is the spell of the thunder-cloud.

No button or seam has my white coat –
This is the spell of the leaping goat.

I can cheat strangers with never a word –
This is the spell of the cuckoo-bird.

We have tongues in plenty but speak no names –
This is the spell of the fiery flames.

The creaking door has a spell to riddle –
I play a tune without any fiddle.

JAMES REEVES

To Every Thing There Is a Season

To every thing there is a season,
 and a time to every purpose under the heaven:
a time to be born,
 and a time to die;
a time to plant,
 and a time to pluck up that which is planted;
a time to kill,
 and a time to heal;
a time to break down,
 and a time to build up;
a time to weep,
 and a time to laugh;
a time to mourn,
 and a time to dance;
a time to cast away stones,
 and a time to gather stones together;

a time to embrace,

    and a time to refrain from embracing;

a time to get,

    and a time to lose;

a time to keep,

    and a time to cast away;

a time to rend,

    and a time to sew;

a time to keep silence,

    and a time to speak;

a time to love,

    and a time to hate;

a time of war,

    and a time of peace.

ECCLESIASTES III, I–VIII

O What Is That Sound

O what is that sound which so thrills the ear
    Down in the valley, drumming, drumming?
Only the scarlet soldiers, dear,
        The soldiers coming.

O what is that light I see flashing so clear
    Over the distance brightly, brightly?
Only the sun on their weapons, dear,
        As they step lightly.

O what are they doing with all that gear;
    What are they doing this morning, this morning?
Only the usual manoeuvres, dear,
        Or perhaps a warning.

O why have they left the road down there;
    Why are they suddenly wheeling, wheeling?
Perhaps a change in the orders, dear;
        Why are you kneeling?

O haven't they stopped for the doctor's care;
    Haven't they reined their horses, their horses?
Why, they are none of them wounded, dear,
        None of these forces.

O is it the parson they want with white hair,
  Is it the parson, is it, is it?
No, they are passing his gateway, dear,
      Without a visit.

O it must be the farmer who lives so near;
  It must be the farmer so cunning, so cunning?
They have passed the farm already, dear,
      And now they are running.

O where are you going? Stay with me here!
  Were the vows you swore me deceiving, deceiving?
No, I promised to love you, dear,
      But I must be leaving.

O it's broken the lock and splintered the door,
  O it's the gate where they're turning, turning;
Their feet are heavy on the floor
      And their eyes are burning.

W. H. Auden

Chess

Said the King with his eye on the enemy's shore,
"I'll declare war."

Said the Queen who possessed a superior brain,
"I'll plan the campaign."

Said the wide-moated Castle with walls all around,
"I'm safe and sound."

Said the Bishop, "We'll lose every battle unless
I pray for success."

Said the Knight on his charger, "I'll carry the day
Or gallop away."

Said the pawn who was born to be soldier and slave,
"I'll go to my grave."

JULIA DONALDSON

People Equal

Some people shoot up tall.
Some hardly leave the ground at all.
    Yet – people equal. Equal.

One voice is a sweet mango.
Another is a non-sugar tomato.
    Yet – people equal. Equal.

Some people rush to the front.
Others hang back, feeling they can't.
    Yet – people equal. Equal.

Hammer some people, you meet a wall.
Blow hard on others they fall.
    Yet – people equal. Equal.

One person will aim at a star.
For another, a hilltop is *too far*.
    Yet – people equal. Equal.

Some people get on with their show.
Others never get on the go.
    Yet – people equal. Equal.

JAMES BERRY

If All the Seas

If all the seas were one sea,
What a great sea that would be!

If all the trees were one tree,
What a great tree that would be!

And if all the axes were one axe,
What a great axe that would be!

And if all the men were one man,
What a great man that would be!

And if the great man took the great axe
And cut down the great tree,

And let it fall into the great sea,
What a splish-splash that would be!

ANON

Give and Take

I give you clean air
You give me poisonous gas.
I give you mountains
You give me quarries.

I give you pure snow
You give me acid rain.
I give you spring fountains
You give me toxic canals.

I give you a butterfly
You gave me a plastic bottle.
I give you a blackbird
You gave me a stealth bomber.

I give you abundance
You give me waste.
I give you one last chance
You give me excuse after excuse.

ROGER MCGOUGH

The Treasures

Who will bring me the hush of a feather?
"I," screeched the Barn Owl. "Whatever the weather."

Who will bring me the shadows that flow?
"I," snarled the Tiger. "Wherever I go."

Who will bring me the colours that shine?
"I," shrieked the Peacock. "Because they are mine."

Who will bring me the crash of the wave?
"I," sang the Dolphin. "Because I am brave."

Who will bring me the secrets of night?
"I," called the Bat. "By the moon's silver light."

Who will bring me the scent of the flower?
"I," hummed the Bee. "By the sun's golden power."

Who will bring me the waterfall's gleam?
"I," sighed the Minnow. "By river and stream."

Who will bring me the strength of the small?
"I," cried the Spider. "When webs line your wall."

Who will bring me the shiver of snow?
"I," howled the Wolf Cub. "When icicles grow."

And who will bring me a nest, furry warm?
"I," squeaked the Rat, "When we hide from the storm . . .
But who will care for the treasures we give?"

"I," said the Child.
"For as long as I live."

CLARE BEVAN

From a Railway Carriage

Faster than fairies, faster than witches,
Bridges and houses, hedges and ditches;
And charging along like troops in a battle,
All through the meadows the horses and cattle:
All of the sights of the hill and the plain
Fly as thick as driving rain;
And ever again, in the wink of an eye,
Painted stations whistle by.

Here is a child who clambers and scrambles,
All by himself and gathering brambles;
Here is a tramp who stands and gazes;
And here is the green for stringing the daisies!
Here is a cart run away in the road
Lumping along with man and load;
And here is a mill, and there is a river:
Each a glimpse and gone forever!

R. L. STEVENSON

Where Are You Going, Johnny?

Where are you going, Johnny-Just-For-A-Lark?
I'm going to play football down at the park.

Where are you going, Johnny-Head-In-The-Air?
To ride on the merry-go-round at the fair.

Where are you going, Johnny-Rushing-From-School?
I'm going for a swim in the swimming pool.

Where are you going, Johnny-Licking-Your-Lips?
I'm off to the fish shop to buy fish and chips.

Where are you going, Johnny-Looking-So-Glum?
I'm going into town to go shopping with Mum.

JOHN FOSTER

Conversation Piece

Late again Blenkinsop?

What's the excuse this time?

Not my fault sir.

Whose fault is it then?

Grandma's sir.

Grandma's. What did she do?

She died sir.

Died?

She's seriously dead all right sir.

That makes four grandmothers this term

And all on PE days Blenkinsop.

I know. It's very upsetting sir.

How many grandmothers have you got Blenkinsop?

Grandmothers sir? None sir.

None?

All dead sir.

And what about yesterday Blenkinsop?

What about yesterday sir?

You missed maths.

That was the dentist sir.

The dentist died?

No sir. My teeth sir.

You missed the test Blenkinsop.

I'd been looking forward to it too sir.

Right, line up for PE.

Can't sir.

No such word as can't. Why can't you?

No kit sir.

Where is it?

Home sir.

What's it doing at home?

Not ironed sir.

Couldn't you iron it?

Can't do it sir.

Why not?

My hand sir.

Who usually does it?

Grandma sir.

Why couldn't she do it?

Dead sir.

GARETH OWEN

Blame

Graham, look at Maureen's leg,
She says you tried to tattoo it!
I did, Miss, yes – with my biro,
But Jonathan told me to do it.

Graham, look at Peter's sock,
It's got a burn-hole through it!
It was just an experiment, Miss, with the lens.
Jonathan told me to do it.

Alice's bag is stuck to the floor,
Look, Graham, did you glue it?
Yes, but I never thought it would work,
And Jonathan told me to do it.

Jonathan, what's all this I hear
About you and Graham Prewitt?
Well, Miss, it's really more his fault:
He *tells* me to tell him to do it!

ALLAN AHLBERG

I Don't Want to Go into School

I don't want to go into school today, Mum,
I don't feel like schoolwork today.
Oh, don't make me go into school today, Mum,
Oh, please let me stay home and play.

But you must go to school, my cherub, my lamb.
If you don't it will be a disaster.
How would they manage without you, my sweet,
After all, you are the headmaster!

COLIN MCNAUGHTON

Question Time

How many books have you written?
Have you been writing for years?
Where do you get all the paper?
Where do you get your ideas?

Do you get bumps on your fingers?
Do you get aches in your wrist?
Please can I go to the toilet?
Did you write "Oliver Twist"?

I've got a book about spiders.
I've got a cut on my knee.
I've got an aunt who speaks German.
Gemma keeps tickling me.

Are you quite old? Are you famous?
Are you a millionaire?
I wasn't putting my hand up –
I was just twiddling my hair.

How many plays have you written?
Do you write one every day?
Do you . . . oh dear, I've forgotten
What I was going to say.

Will you be staying to dinner?
Will you go home on the bus?
How many poems have you written?
Will you write one about us?

JULIA DONALDSON

Creative Writing

My story on Monday began:

Mountainous seas crashed on the cliffs,

And the desolate land grew wetter . . .

The teacher wrote a little note: *Remember the capital letter!*

My poem on Tuesday began:

Red tongues of fire

Licked higher and higher

From smoking Etna's top.

The teacher wrote a little note: *Where is your full stop?*

My story on Wednesday began:

Through the lonely, pine-scented wood

There twists a hidden path . . .

The teacher wrote a little note: *Start a paragraph!*

My poem on Thursday began:

The trembling child,

Eyes dark and wild,

Frozen midst the fighting . . .

The teacher wrote a little note: *Take care – untidy writing!*

My story on Friday began:

> *The boxer bruised and bloody lay,*
>
> *His eye half closed and swollen . . .*

The teacher wrote a little note: *Use a semi-colon!*

Next Monday my story will begin:

> *Once upon a time . . .*

GERVASE PHINN

What I Love About School

What I love about school
     is the hurly-burly of the classroom,
     the sly humour of the teachers

What I hate about teachers
     is their reluctance to cartwheel
     down corridors

What I love about corridors
     is that the longer they are
     the louder the echo

What I hate about echo echo
     is its refusal to answer a straight
     question question

What I love about question
     is the proud admission
     of its own ignorance

What I hate about ignorance
     is the naïve assumption
     that it is bliss

What I love about bliss
    is its willingness
    to rhyme with kiss

What I hate about kiss
    is the news of it going around
    like wildfire

What I love about wildfire
    is its dragon's breath
    and its hunger for life

What I hate about life
    is that as soon as you get the hang of it
    you run out of time

What I love about time
    is how it flies
    except when at school

What I hate about school
    is the hurly-burly of the playground,
    the sly humour of the teachers.

ROGER McGOUGH

Instructions for Giants

Please do not step on swing parks, youth clubs,
    cinemas or discos.
Please flatten all schools!

Please do not eat children, pop stars, TV soap actors,
    kind grannies who give us 50p.
Please feel free to gobble up dentists and teachers
    any time you like!

Please do not block out the sunshine.
Please push all rain clouds over to France.

Please do not drink the public swimming pool.
Please eat all cabbage fields, vegetable plots
        and anything green that grows in the
            boring countryside!

Please do not trample kittens, lambs or other baby animals.
Please take spiders and snakes, ants and beetles home for
   your own pets.

Please stand clear of the jets passing.
Please sew up the ozone layer.
Please mind where you're put your big feet! –
and no sneaking off to China when we're playing
   hide and seek.

JOHN RICE

Boys' Game?

"This is our side of the playground,
What are you doing here?
You want to play football?
That's a laugh!
It's a boys' game. Got it clear?"

"Actually, Kev, she's pretty good,
Especially in goal.
I saw her down the rec last night:
She was really in control.
Saved a penalty early on,
And from corners . . . can't she catch!
Dived several times
At their striker's feet —
Really kept us in the match."
"Well, in that case . . .
Of course, it's actually
In goal where we're really weak.

I mean, anyone's got to be better
Than Baggs —
He couldn't play hide-and-seek.
Even a girl would be better than him.
Look, we've got to decide.
Let's take her on.
Hey, where's she gone . . .?
Oh, she's gone back to their side."

ERIC FINNEY

Football Mad

Oh no, bless my soul!
Clever Trevor's scored a goal.

So he runs up the pitch
And wriggles his botty,
He is kissed by ten men
All sweaty and snotty,
Now he's waving his fist
To the Queen who just stares
The lad's going crazy
But everyone cheers.
Now what's he doing?
He's chewing the cud!
Now what's he doing?
He's rolling in mud!
Now he is crying
I think he's in pain
Now what's he doing?
He's smiling again.

Oh no, bless my soul
Clever Trevor's scored a goal.

He's doing gymnastics
He's doing some mime
He's kissing the ground
For a very long time,
He's now on his back
With his feet in the air
Now he's gone all religious
And stopped for a prayer.
Did he pray for the sick?
Did he pray for the poor?
No, he prayed for the ball
And he prayed to score.
No one but no one
Can re-start the game
Until Trevor has had
His moment of fame.

Oh no, bless my soul
Clever Trevor's scored a goal,
He kicked the ball into the net
How much money will he get?

BENJAMIN ZEPHANIAH

London 2012

Pulses racing,
Athletes pacing.

Flags flapping,
Crowds clapping.

Hearts pounding,
Starting-guns sounding.

Swimmers swimming,
Glasses brimming.

Cameras flashing,
Cyclists crashing.

Adrenalin pumping,
Jumpers jumping.

Anthems playing,
Banners swaying.

Medals gleaming,
Children screaming.

London's waiting,
We're celebrating . . .

LONDON 2012!

CIARÁN POWDERS

The Dinosaur Rap

Come on, everybody, shake a claw.
Let's hear you bellow, let's hear you roar.
Let's hear you thump and clump and clap.
Come and join in. Do the dinosaur rap.

There's a young T-Rex over by the door
Who's already stamped a hole in the floor.

There's a whirling, twirling apatosaurus
Encouraging everyone to join in the chorus.

Come on, everybody, shake a claw.
Let's hear you bellow, let's hear you roar.
Let's hear you thump and clump and clap.
Come and join in. Do the dinosaur rap.

There's a stegosaurus rattling his spines
And an iguanodon making thumbs-up signs.

There's an allosaurus giving a shout
As he thrashes and lashes his tail about.

Come on, everybody, shake a claw.
Let's hear you bellow. Let's hear you roar.
Let's hear you thump and clump and clap.
Come and join in. Do the dinosaur rap.

There's a triceratops who can't stop giggling
At the way her partner's writhing and wriggling.

There's an ankylosaurus swaying to the beat,
Clomping and clumping and stomping his feet.

There are dinosaurs here. There are dinosaurs there.
There are dinosaurs dancing everywhere.
So swing your tails and shake your claws.
Join in the rapping with the dinosaurs.

JOHN FOSTER

Hands

One, two,
What can you do?

We can . . .

Stroke a cat,
Put on a hat,

Shake your hand,
Dig in the sand.

Drive a car,
Play the guitar,

Scrub the floor,
Knock on the door,

Turn a screw,
Tie up a shoe,

Toot the flute,
Pull off a boot,

Brush your hair,
Cuddle a bear,

Wave goodnight
And switch out the light.

JULIA DONALDSON

Queue for the Zoo

Oh no! There's a queue!
What shall we do?
Act like the animals
In the zoo . . .

Growl like tigers,
Grizzle like bears,
Skip about like
Mad March Hares,
Squirm like snakes,
And squeak like rats,
Flap our coats
Like vampire bats,
Jump as high as
A kangaroo . . .

I'm glad we're in a queue –
Aren't you?

CLARE BEVAN

Worm Words

"Keep still!"
said Big Worm
to Little Worm.
"You're driving me
round the bend."

"Don't be daft,"
said Little Worm.
"I'm your other end."

TONY MITTON

What a Shame You Lost Your Tail

"What a shame
you humans
lost your tail," said Monkey.

You could have been doing like me
and swinging from tree to tree.

"What a shame
you humans
lost your tail," said Dog.

Now, that's a drag,
when friends come you got nothing to wag.

"What a shame
you humans
lost your tail," said Lizard.

If I break mine, no bother,
I can always grow back another.

"What a shame
you humans
lost your tail," said Coyote.

In the beginning when fire was rare and earth dark,
it was my tricky brush that stole the magic spark.

"What a shame
you humans
lost your tail," said Anaconda.

When I crush a body till the final squeal,
what a joy to coil myself around my meal.

"What a shame
you humans
lost your tail," said Pig.

My curly stump,
sure adds a touch to my old rump.

"What a shame
you humans
lost your tail," said Beaver.

Moving through water is easy to handle
When you're born with a ready-made paddle.

"We know we lost our tail," said the humans.

But we have a bottom, a bum, a rear,
call it what you will.
It's good for sitting on
to improve our thinking skill.

"Yes, we lost our tail,"
Said the humans once again.
"But we have a brain
and we make things that heal and things

that kill."

JOHN AGARD

The Three-Headed Dog

Dog 1: I'm Nip.
Dog 2: I'm Ripper.
Dog 3: My name is Guss.
All: We are the monster called Cerberus!

Dog 1: I'm feeling hungry.
Dog 2: I like to howl.
Dog 3: I've found the dinner bowl.
All: Growl! Growl! Growl!

Dog 1: I'm chewing gristle.
Dog 2: I like to whine.
Dog 3: I've grabbed the greasy bits.
All: Mine! Mine! Mine!

Dog 1: I'm sniffing tree trunks.
Dog 2: I like a nap.
Dog 3: I'm gnawing rabbit bones.
All: Yap! Yap! Yap!

Dog 1: I'm smelling danger.
Dog 2: I like the dark.
Dog 3: I'm hearing sneaky feet.
All: Bark! Bark! Bark!

Dog 1:	I've caught a burglar.
Dog 2:	I like to fight.
Dog 3:	I've pinned him to the ground.
All:	Bite! Bite! Bite!

Dog 1:	We are the winners.
Dog 2:	We like to score.
Dog 3:	We're feeling sleepy now.
All:	Snore! Snore! Snore!

Dog 1:	I'm Nip.
Dog 2:	I'm Ripper.
Dog 3:	My name is Guss.
All:	We are the monster called CER – BER – US!!

CLARE BEVAN

The Blind Men and the Elephant

It was six men of Hindostan,
　　To learning much inclined,
Who went to see the elephant,
　　(Though all of them were blind)
That each by observation
　　Might satisfy his mind.

The *first* approached the Elephant,
　　And happening to fall
Against his broad and sturdy side,
　　At once began to bawl:
"Bless me, it seems the Elephant
　　Is very like a wall."

The *second*, feeling of his tusk,
　　Cried, "Ho! What have we here
So very round and smooth and sharp?
　　To me 'tis mighty clear
This wonder of an Elephant
　　Is very like a spear."

The *third* approached the animal,
    And happening to take
The squirming trunk within his hands,
    Then boldly up and spake:
"I see," quoth he, "the Elephant
    Is very like a snake."

The *fourth* stretched out his eager hand
    And felt about the knee,
"What most this mighty beast is like
    Is mighty plain; quoth he;
"'Tis clear enough the Elephant
    Is very like a tree."

The *fifth* who chanced to touch the ear
    Said, "Even the blindest man
Can tell what this resembles most;
    Deny the fact who can,
This marvel of an Elephant
    Is very like a fan."

The *sixth* no sooner had begun
　　About the beast to grope,
Than, seizing on the swinging tail
　　That fell within his scope,
"I see," cried he, "the Elephant
　　Is very like a rope."

And so these men of Hindostan
　　Disputed loud and long,
Each in his own opinion
　　Exceeding stiff and strong,
Though *each* was *partly* in the right
　　And all were in the wrong.

JOHN GODFREY SAXE

A Nail

For want of a nail, the shoe was lost;
For want of a shoe, the horse was lost;
For want of a horse, the rider was lost;
For want of a rider, the battle was lost;
For want of a battle, the kingdom was lost:
And all for want of a horseshoe nail.

ANON

The Blind Dog

My kindly human sighs for me,
But with my clever nose I see . . .

The perfumed path of a lady dog,
The fishy trail of a passing frog,
The sharp, clear stink of a scavenging fox,
The tempting scents of a cardboard box,

The glorious odours of dustbin day,
The tang of a lamp-post in my way,
The feathery whiff of a broken bird,
The traces of ice cream, softly blurred,

The insults left by an old tom cat,
The slimy tracks of a sewer rat,
The homely smell of our garden gate,
The call of the gravy on my plate.

My kindly human sighs for me,
But with my clever nose – I see.

CLARE BEVAN

90

Conversation

Mousie, mousie,
Where is your little wee housie?
    Here is the door,
    Under the floor,
        Said mousie, mousie.

Mousie, mousie,
May I come into your housie?
    You can't get in,
    You have to be thin,
        Said mousie, mousie.

Mousie, mousie,
Won't you come out of your housie?
    I'm sorry to say
    I'm busy all day,
        Said mousie, mousie.

ROSE FYLEMAN

Rum Tum Tugger

The Rum Tum Tugger is a Curious Cat:
If you offer him pheasant he would rather have grouse.
If you put him in a house he would much prefer a flat,
If you put him in a flat then he'd rather have a house.
If you set him on a mouse then he only wants a rat,
If you set him on a rat then he'd rather chase a mouse.
Yes the Rum Tum Tugger is a Curious Cat —
    And there isn't any call for me to shout it:
       For he will do
       As he do do
         And there's no doing anything about it!

The Rum Tum Tugger is a terrible bore:
When you let him in, then he wants to be out;
He's always on the wrong side of every door,
And as soon as he's at home, then he'd like to get about.
He likes to lie in the bureau drawer,
But he makes such a fuss if he can't get out.
Yet the Rum Tum Tugger is a Curious Cat —
    And it isn't any use for you to doubt it:
      For he will do
      As he do do
        And there's no doing anything about it!

The Rum Tum Tugger is a curious beast:
His disobliging ways are a matter of habit.
If you offer him fish then he always wants a feast;
When there isn't any fish then he won't eat rabbit.
If you offer him cream then he sniffs and sneers,
For he only likes what he finds for himself;
So you'll catch him in it right up to his ears,
If you put it away on the larder shelf.

The Rum Tum Tugger is artful and knowing,

The Rum Tum Tugger doesn't care for a cuddle;

But he'll leap on your lap in the middle of your sewing,

For there's nothing he enjoys like a horrible muddle.

Yes the Rum Tum Tugger is a Curious Cat —

    And there isn't any need for me to spout it:

        For he will do

        As he do do

           And there's no doing anything about it!

T. S. ELIOT

Cats

Cats sleep
Anywhere,
Any table,
Any chair,
Top of piano,
Window-ledge,
In the middle,
On the edge,
Open drawer,
Empty shoe,
Anybody's
Lap will do,
Fitted in a
Cardboard box,
In the cupboard
With your frocks –
Anywhere!
They don't care!
Cats sleep
Anywhere.

ELEANOR FARJEON

Cows

Half the time they munched the grass, and all the
    time they lay
Down in the water-meadows, the lazy month of May,
        A-chewing,
        A-mooing,
    To pass the hours away.

        "Nice weather," said the brown cow.
            "Ah," said the white.
        "Grass is very tasty."
            "Grass is all right."

Half the time they munched the grass, and all the
    time they lay
Down in the water-meadows, the lazy month of May,
        A-chewing,
        A-mooing,
    To pass the hours away.

        "Rain coming," said the brown cow.
            "Ah," said the white.
        "Flies is very tiresome."
            "Flies bite."

Half the time they munched the grass, and all the
time they lay
Down in the water-meadows, the lazy month of May,
A-chewing,
A-mooing,
To pass the hours away.

"Time to go," said the brown cow.
"Ah," said the white.
"Nice chat." "Very pleasant."
"Night." "Night."

Half the time they munched the grass, and all the
time they lay
Down in the water-meadows, the lazy month of May,
A-chewing,
A-mooing,
To pass the hours away.

JAMES REEVES

Don't Call Alligator Long-Mouth Till You Cross River

Call alligator long-mouth
call alligator saw-mouth
call alligator pushy-mouth
call alligator scissors-mouth
call alligator raggedy-mouth
call alligator bumpy-bum
call alligator all dem rude word
but better wait

          till you cross river.

JOHN AGARD

Trading

Went to the river, couldn't get across,
Paid five dollars for an old gray hoss.
Hoss wouldn't pull so I traded for a bull.
Bull wouldn't holler so I traded for a dollar.
Dollar wouldn't pass so I threw it on the grass.
Grass wouldn't grow so I traded for a hoe.
Hoe wouldn't dig so I traded for a pig.
Pig wouldn't squeal so I traded for a wheel.
Wheel wouldn't run so I traded for a gun.
Gun wouldn't shoot so I traded for a boot.
Boot wouldn't fit so I thought I'd better quit.
So I quit.

TRADITIONAL AMERICAN

Pirate Pete

Pirate Pete
had a ship on the sea
had a fish for his tea
had a peg for a knee

　and a tiny little parrot called . . . Polly.

Pirate Pete
had a book with a map
had a skull on his cap
had a cat on his lap

　and another little parrot called . . . Dolly.

Pirate Pete
had a trunk full of treasure
had a belt made of leather
had a cap with a feather

　and another little parrot called . . . Jolly

Pirate Pete
had a patch on his eye
had a flag he would fly
had a plank way up high

   and another little parrot called . . . Molly

So Pirate Pete
and the parrots four
they sailed the world
from shore to shore –
collecting gold
and gifts galore.
And that's their tale –
there is no more!

JAMES CARTER

Overheard on a Saltmarsh

Nymph, nymph, what are your beads?

Green glass, goblin. Why do you stare at them?

Give them me.

        No.

Give them me.   Give them me.

           No.

Then I will howl all night in the reeds,
Lie in the mud and howl for them.

Goblin, why do you love them so?

They are better than stars or water,
Better than voices of winds that sing,
Better than any man's fair daughter,
Your green glass beads on a silver ring.

Hush, I stole them out of the moon.

Give me your beads, I want them.

                                        No.

I will howl in a deep lagoon
For your green glass beads, I love them so.
Give them me. Give them me.

                            No.

                    HAROLD MUNRO

Arabian Nights

Here is a ring
(make ring out of index finger and thumb)

on a silver dish.
(place it on open palm)

Put it on your finger
(put ring on other index finger)

and make a wish.
(throw hands open in wonder)

Here is a genie
who waits in a flask.
(cup both hands, thumbs apart)

If you want a favour
(mime whisper into thumb gap)
whisper and ask.

Here is a carpet
(open hand, palm upwards)
that knows how to fly.

Climb on. Sit tight.
(walk first two fingers of other hand onto carpet and pause)

Up into the sky!
(raise carpet, take-off!)

Tony Mitton

Witch, Witch

"Witch, witch, where do you fly?" . . .
"Under the clouds and over the sky."

"Witch, witch, what do you eat?" . . .
"Little black apples from Hurricane Street."

"Witch, witch, what do you drink?" . . .
"Vinegar, blacking and good red ink."

"Witch, witch, where do you sleep?" . . .
"Up in the clouds where pillows are cheap."

ROSE FYLEMAN

The Dark Wood

In the dark, dark wood there was
     a dark, dark house,
And in that dark, dark house, there was
     a dark, dark room,
And in that dark, dark room there was
     a dark, dark cupboard,
And in that dark, dark cupboard there was
     a dark, dark shelf,
And on that dark, dark shelf there was
     a dark, dark box,
And in that dark, dark box there was a
     GHOST!

ANON

The Visitor

A crumbling churchyard, the sea and the moon;
The waves had gouged out grave and bone;
A man was walking, late and alone . . .

He saw a skeleton on the ground;
A ring on a bony hand he found.

He ran home to his wife and gave her the ring.
"Oh, where did you get it?" He said not a thing.

"It's the loveliest ring in the world," she said.
As it glowed on her finger. They skipped off to bed.

At midnight they woke. In the dark outside,
"Give me my ring!" a chill voice cried.

"What was that, William? What did it say?"
"Don't worry, my dear. It'll soon go away."

"I'm coming!" A skeleton opened the door.
"Give me my ring!" It was crossing the floor.

"What was that, William? What did it say?"
"Don't worry, my dear. It'll soon go away."

"I'm reaching you now! I'm climbing the bed."
The wife pulled the sheet right over her head.

It was torn from her grasp and tossed in the air:
"I'll drag you out of bed by the hair!"

"What was that, William? What did it say?"
"Throw the ring through the window! THROW IT AWAY!"

She threw it. The skeleton leapt from the sill,
Scooped up the ring and clattered downhill,
Fainter . . . and fainter . . . Then all was still.

IAN SERRAILLIER

This Is the Key to the Castle

This is the key to the castle.

This is the box
with rusty locks
that holds the key to the castle.

This is the spider, huge and fat,
who wove its web and sat and sat
on top of the box
with rusty locks
that holds the key to the castle.

This is the cellar, cold and bare,
dark as a grave, with nothing there
except the spider, huge and fat,
who wove its web and sat and sat
on top of the box
with rusty locks
that holds the key to the castle.

This is the stair that crumbles and creaks
where every small step moans and squeaks
that leads to the cellar, cold and bare,
dark as the grave, with nobody there

except the spider, huge and fat,
who wove its web and sat and sat
on top of the box
with rusty locks
that holds the key to the castle.

This is the rat with yellow teeth,
sharp as sorrow, long as grief,
who ran up the stair that crumbles and creaks
where every small step moans and squeaks
up from the cellar, cold and bare,
dark as the grave, with nobody there
except the spider, huge and fat,
who wove its web and sat and sat
on top of the box
with rusty locks
that holds the key to the castle.

This is the damp and dirty hall
with peeling paper on its mouldy wall
where the black rat runs with yellow teeth
sharp as sorrow, long as grief,
who ran up the stair that crumbles and creaks
up from the cellar, cold and bare,
dark as a grave, with nobody there
except the spider, huge and fat,
who wove its web and sat and sat
on top of the box
with rusty locks
that holds the key to the castle.

This is the ghost with rattling bones,
carrying his head, whose horrible groans
fill the damp and dirty hall
with peeling paper on its mouldy wall
where the black rat runs with yellow teeth
sharp as sorrow, long as grief,
who ran up the stair that crumbles and creaks
up from the cellar, cold and bare,
dark as the grave, with nobody there
except the spider, huge and fat,

who wove its web and sat and sat
on top of the box
with rusty locks
that holds the key to the castle.

This is the child who came in to play
on a rainy, windy, nasty day
and said BOO! to the ghost who groaned in the hall
and SCAT! to the rat by the mouldy wall
and went down the creaking crumbling stair
into the cellar, cold and bare,
and laughed at the spider, huge and fat,
and brushed off the web where it sat and sat
and opened the box
with the rusty locks
and took the key to the castle.

DAVE CALDER

There Was An Old Lady

There was an old lady who swallowed a fly.
I don't know why she swallowed a fly.
Perhaps she'll die.

There was an old lady who swallowed a spider
That wriggled and jiggled and tickled inside her.
She swallowed the spider to catch the fly;
I don't know why she swallowed a fly.
Perhaps she'll die.

There was an old lady who swallowed a bird.
How absurd to swallow a bird!
She swallowed the bird to catch the spider
That wriggled and jiggled and tickled inside her.
She swallowed the spider to catch the fly;
I don't know why she swallowed a fly.
Perhaps she'll die.

There was an old lady who swallowed a cat.
Fancy that! She swallowed a cat.
She swallowed the cat to catch the bird,
She swallowed the bird to catch the spider
That wriggled and jiggled and tickled inside her.
She swallowed the spider to catch the fly;
I don't know why she swallowed a fly.
Perhaps she'll die.

There was an old lady who swallowed a dog.
What a hog to swallow a dog!

She swallowed the dog to catch the cat,
She swallowed the cat to catch the bird,
She swallowed the bird to catch the spider
That wriggled and jiggled and tickled inside her.
She swallowed the spider to catch the fly;
I don't know why she swallowed a fly.
Perhaps she'll die!

There was an old lady who swallowed a cow.
I don't know how she swallowed a cow!
She swallowed the cow to catch the dog,
She swallowed the dog to catch the cat,
She swallowed the cat to catch the bird,
She swallowed the bird to catch the spider
That wriggled and jiggled and tickled inside her.
She swallowed the spider to catch the fly;
I don't know why she swallowed a fly.
Perhaps she'll die!

There was an old lady who swallowed a horse . . .

She's dead, of course!

ANON

A B C Ma Grannie Found a Flea

A B C ma grannie found a flea
She salted it and peppered it and had it for her tea.

A B C and D E F ma grannie went deaf
Goin to the football and shoutin at the ref.

D E F and G H I ma grannie made a pie
Bluebottle biscuits and bread-and-butterfly.

G H I and J K L ma grannie made a smell
What did she smell like? Not very well.

J K L and M N O ma grannie broke her toe
They put her in the hospital, they wouldny let her go.

M N O and P Q R ma grannie bought a car
She took us out for hurlies on the handlebar.

P Q R and S T U ma grannie caught the flu
Doin the Hokey Cokey wi a kangaroo.

S T U and V W ma grannie turned blue
We put her in the bed and we cried Boo Hoo.

But X Y Z ma grannie wasny dead
So instead of getting buried she got married instead.

EWAN MCVICAR

*The verse "A B C ma grannie found a flea, She salted it and peppered it
and had it for her tea" is 'traditional', from Glasgow.*

The Trouble with My Brother

Thomas was only three
And though he was not fat
We knew that there was something wrong
When he ate the cat.

Nibble, nibble, munch, munch,
Nibble, nibble, munch,
Nibble, nibble, munch, munch,
He had the cat for lunch!

He ate a lump of coal,
He ate a candlestick
And when he ate the tortoise
Mother felt quite sick.

Nibble, nibble, munch, munch,
Nibble, nibble, munch,
Nibble, nibble, munch, munch,
A tortoise for lunch!

When he was a boy of four
He went to the zoo by bus
And alarmed us all by eating
A hippopotamus.

Nibble, nibble, munch, munch,
Nibble, nibble, munch,
Nibble, nibble, munch, munch,
A hippopotamus for lunch!

When he went to school
We tried to warn the teacher
But Thomas pounced long before
Anyone could reach her.

Nibble, nibble, munch, munch,
Nibble, nibble, munch,
Nibble, nibble, munch, munch,
A teacher for lunch!

We used to get nice letters
So mum was full of grief
When upon the doorstep
She found the postman's teeth.

Nibble, nibble, munch, munch,
Nibble, nibble, munch,
Nibble, nibble, munch, munch,
A postman for lunch!

He ate thirteen baby-sitters
(We often heard their squeals)
He ate a social worker
In between these meals.

Nibble, nibble, munch, munch,
Nibble, nibble, munch,
Nibble, nibble, munch, munch,
A social worker for lunch!

A policeman came to have a word
About what was going on,
Thomas took a shine to him
And soon he was all gone.

Nibble, nibble, munch, munch,
Nibble, nibble, munch,
Nibble, nibble, munch, munch,
A policeman for lunch!

None of us says much,
It holds us all in thrall,
Having a little brother
Who is a cannibal.

Nibble, nibble, munch, munch,
Nibble, nibble, munch.
At supper time we hide away,
Nibble, nibble, munch!

Brian Patten

Tea with Aunty Mabel

If you ever go to tea with my Aunty Mabel,
Never put your elbows on the dining-room table,
Always wipe your shoes if you've been in the garden,
Don't ever burp. If you do, say pardon.
Don't put your feet on the new settee,
If she offers you a sugar lump, don't take three.
Don't dunk your biscuits, don't make crumbs,
Don't bite nails and don't suck thumbs.
Don't rock the budgie, don't tease the peke,
Speak when you're spoken to or else don't speak.
Do as you're told and if you're not able,
Don't go to tea with my Aunty Mabel.

JEANNE WILLIS

122

Mrs Mason's Basin

Mrs Mason bought a basin,
Mrs Tyson said, "What a nice 'un,"
"What did it cost?" said Mrs Frost,
"Half a crown," said Mrs Brown,
"Did it indeed," said Mrs Reed,
"It did for certain," said Mrs Burton.
Then Mrs Nix up to her tricks
Threw the basin on the bricks.

ANON

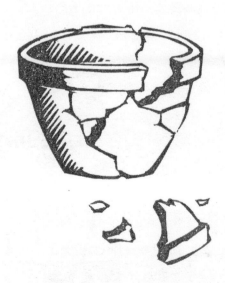

I've Got a Ball of Pastry

I've got a ball of pastry.
What shall I do with that?
You've got to roll it, roll it, roll it,
Until you've rolled that pastry flat.

I've got a ripe banana.
Tell me where I begin.
You've got to peel it, peel it, peel it,
Until you've peeled off all the skin.

I've got a pot of porridge,
Creamy and thick and hot.
You've got to stir it, stir it, stir it,
Until it's bubbling in the pot.

I've got a jar of strawberry jam,
Sticky and sweet and red.
You've got to spread it, spread it, spread it,
Until it's on a slice of bread.

I've got a flat round pancake.
One side has just been fried.
You've got to toss it, toss it, toss it,
Until it lands the other side.

I've got a round brown walnut.
Tell me what I should do.
You've got to crack it, crack it, crack it,
Until you've cracked the shell in two.

I've got a plate of dinner.
What do you think that's for?
You've got to eat it, eat it, eat it,
And if it's nice you'll ask for more.

JULIA DONALDSON

Dinner-Time Rhyme

Can you tell me, if you please,
Who it is likes mushy peas?

Louise likes peas.

How about Sam?
  Sam likes spam.

How about Vince?
  Vince likes mince.

How about Kelly?
  Kelly likes jelly.

How about Trish?
  Trish likes fish.

How about Pips?
  Pips likes chips.

How about Pete?
  Pete likes meat.

How about Sue?
    Sue likes stew.

How about Greg?
    Greg likes egg.

How about Pam?
    Pam likes lamb.

OK, then, tell me, if you can –
How about Katerina Wilhelmina Theodora Dobson?

    She goes home for dinner . . .

JUNE CREBBIN

Yellow Butter

Yellow butter, purple jelly, red jam, black bread.

Spread it thick,
Say it quick,

Yellow butter, purple jelly, red jam, black bread.

Spread it thicker,
Say it quicker,

Yellow butter, purple jelly, red jam, black bread.

Now repeat it,
While you eat it,

Yellow butter, purple jelly, red jam, black bread . . .

Don't talk
With your mouth full!

MARY ANN HOBERMAN

The Food Train

Cof-fee, cof-fee, cof-fee, cof-fee.
Bread and butter, bread and butter, bread and butter,
    bread and butter,
Biscuits and cheese, biscuits and cheese, biscuits and cheese,
    biscuits and cheese,
Fish and chips, fish and chips, fish and chips, fish and chips
    fish and chips, fish and chips, fish and chips, fish and chips,
SOUP!

JULIA DONALDSON

129

I Know Someone

I know someone who can
take a mouthful of custard and blow it
down their nose.
I know someone who can
make their ears wiggle.
I know someone who can
shake their cheeks so it sounds
like ducks quacking.
I know someone who can
throw peanuts in the air and catch them
in their mouth.
I know someone who can
balance a pile of 12 2p pieces on his elbow
and snatch his elbow from under them
and catch them.
I know someone who can
bend her thumb back to touch her wrist.
I know someone who can
crack his nose.

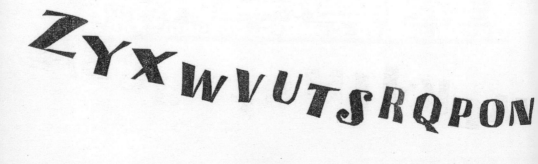

I know someone who can
say the alphabet backwards.
I know someone who can
put their hands in
their armpits and blow raspberries.
I know someone who can
wiggle her little toe.
I know someone who can
lick the bottom of her chin.
I know someone who can
slide their top lip one way
and their bottom lip the other way,
and that someone is
ME.

MICHAEL ROSEN

MLKJIHGFEDCBA

Today, I Feel

Today, I feel as:

Pleased as PUNCH,
Fit as a FIDDLE,
Keen as a KNIFE,
Hot as a GRIDDLE,
Bold as BRASS,
Bouncy as a BALL,
Keen as MUSTARD,
High as a WALL,
Bright as a BUTTON,
Light as a FEATHER,
Fresh as a DAISY,
Fragrant as HEATHER,
Chirpy as a CRICKET,
Sound as a BELL,
Sharp as a NEEDLE,
Deep as a WELL,
High as a KITE,
Strong as a BULL,
Bubbly as BATH WATER,
Warm as WOOL,
Clean as a NEW PIN,
Shiny as MONEY,

Quick as LIGHTNING,
Sweet as HONEY,
Cool as a CUCUMBER,
Fast as a HARE,
Right as RAIN,
Brave as a BEAR,
Lively as a MONKEY,
Busy as a BEE,
Good as GOLD,
Free as the SEA.

I'M SO HAPPY – I'M JUST LOST FOR WORDS.

GERVASE PHINN

Sshhhhhh!

Sshhhhhh!
Don't russhh
Or the fox will be off
With a swisshh
Of its brusshh.

Hushhh!
Don't splasshh
Or the shhimering fisshh
Will be gone in a flasshh.

Shusshh!
Don't crasshh
Or the sshhy thrusshh
That sings in the busshh
Will vanisshhhhhh.
The song
Will
Finisshhhhhhhh.

JULIA DONALDSON

Suggestions for Performance

All the poems in this book are suitable to be performed by more than one voice, but there are any number of ways in which individual poems might be presented. Some poems may work best simply recited by pairs or groups of children, others lend themselves to simple actions, mime, or even more elaborate staging with props and costumes. Here are a few of my suggestions to start you off:

A B C Ma Grannie Found a Flea
The class can be divided into nine groups, each one to recite a verse.

Arabian Nights
Any number of children can recite this together, while they perform the hand gestures described in the poem.

Blame
A poem for just three voices – the teacher, Graham and Jonathan – although other children could take the non-speaking roles of Maureen, Peter and Alice.

The Blind Dog
The whole class can recite the first and last couplets, while the other lines are divided up.

The Blind Men and the Elephant
One child can narrate (this is quite a demanding role), or one child can speak the first and last verses, while each of the other verses is spoken by a different child. Meanwhile six others are the six blind men, who mime groping about and touching different parts of the elephant.

Boys' Game?
This is a dialogue between two boys, but a girl needs to take part as well for it to make sense. Even though the girl has no lines, she can dribble a football and then run off at the end.

Caribbean Counting Poem
Divide the class into nine groups, each to recite one verse, with the whole class doing the last verse. There is also scope for movement and action in this poem, or perhaps for artwork to be displayed by each group.

Cats
The whole class can recite the first two and the last two lines, while the rest of the poem is divided up between individuals, or pairs of voices.

Chess
Six children speak the lines of the six different chess pieces. The narration can either be recited by all six, or else by the whole class.

Conversation
Two voices are needed here, or else a class could chant the questions and the narration, while an individual acts the mouse.

Conversation Piece
This is best performed by just two children, one acting the teacher and the other being Blenkinsop.

Cows
Two children act the brown cow and the white cow while the class recites the chorus.

Creative Writing
This can either be performed by two children (one being the child, the other reciting "The teacher wrote a little note" and also acting the teacher.) Alternatively, five different children could be chosen to be the story-writer for each day of the week, with five more children voicing the teacher's comments. In that case, all the "story-writers" could speak the last two lines together.

The Dark Wood

Divide up the first six lines. Each one should be spoken more softly than the one before. The seventh line can be whispered, until the last word, "GHOST!", which can be shouted by the whole class.

Dinner-Time Rhyme

This can be spoken by two children (one asking, the other answering the questions) or ten children can speak the answers, with them all joining in to say the final line together.

The Dinosaur Rap

The whole class chants the chorus, with the verses being divided up between individuals. This poem would lend itself well to some movement or actions.

Don't Call Alligator Long-Mouth Till You Cross River

The first six lines are taken by six different children, and the class chants the ending. It could be fun to act this one out, with someone acting a crocodile snapping at children who attempt to cross the river.

The Food Train

Children could form a train to chant this poem, in which we hear the train speeding up and then going into a tunnel for the final "SOUP!". Or it could perhaps be spoken as a round.

Football Mad

The whole class can speak the chorus "Oh no, bless my soul! Clever Trevor's scored a goal", and the last two lines, with the other lines being divided up between eight or sixteen groups, or solo voices. The performance could be accompanied by a mime of Clever Trevor's antics.

From a Railway Carriage

It could be fun for a group of six or eight children to perform this poem sitting on chairs as if they were in a railway carriage, dividing up the lines, with children pointing out of the imaginary window for the lines which begin "Here is . . ." and the whole group saying the last line.

Give and Take
The poem can be divided into eight pairs of lines, with a single child or a group reading each section.

Hands
This is an action poem, which could be performed by any number of children. If a whole class is doing it, I would suggest that everyone chants the first two and the last two lines and that the rest of the poem is divided between groups or individuals, with appropriate actions.

I Don't Want to Go into School
One child recites Mum's lines, while another one acts the other character (who turns out to be the headmaster).

I Know Someone
Each boast can be spoken by a different child, with the whole class saying the last two lines.

If All the Seas
Four different groups chant the first four couplets. A fifth group does the following four lines, and the whole class shouts the final line. (It could work well if each group is bigger and louder than the one before.)

Instructions for Giants
This can be recited by a group of thirteen or fourteen children, each speaking one of the instructions (the final instruction is probably best divided in two). The children might also like to write some further instructions to giants, or to insects or teachers or parents, and then turn these into another performance poem.

I've Got a Ball of Pastry
Individual children can ask the different questions, and the whole class can provide the answers, with

appropriate actions. Or the poem could be performed by just two children.

The Jumblies
One group of children can be the Jumblies, clustered together as if in a sieve. Another group can be the landlubbers and say the lines spoken by "everyone" in verses 1, 2 and 6. The whole class can chant the chorus "Far and few . . . " etc, and individual children can be chosen, one for each verse, to speak the remaining text.

London 2012
The couplets can be divided up between different voices, with the whole class chanting the last line.

Mrs Mason's Basin
This is fun to act out with seven girls playing the different women and passing a bowl around. The final speaker (Mrs Nix) flings the bowl to the ground.

My Colours
The whole class can start and finish the poem, while the verses about the specific colours are each spoken by a different child or group. If the poem is performed publicly it could be fun if the children wear tops or scarves of the appropriate colour.

My True Love
This could be performed by two children, one acting the "true love" and the other one being the "I" of the poem. Or else the class could be split in two to perform the poem. It could be fun for there to be simple props, or pieces of artwork to represent the gifts.

A Nail
Allocate each line to a different child or group, with the whole class reciting the last line.

Nut Tree

One child can narrate (or the narration can be divided between several children). The rest of the class curl up small and then mime the nut growing into a tree, swaying in the wind, and then shedding leaves and nuts. They finish curled up once more.

O What Is That Sound

Although this could be performed by a whole class, divided into two (one group asking the questions, the other providing the answers), I think it would be more effective with just two voices.

Overheard on a Saltmarsh

Two children are needed to recite this, one playing the nymph (who can wear or hold some green beads), and the other the goblin.

People Equal

The chorus can be chanted by the whole class, with twelve individuals or groups speaking a line each.

Pirate Pete

Someone can dress up as Pirate Pete, and four more children can act the parrots, flying to join Pete when their names are called. Individual children can recite the lines, perhaps bringing on props to give to Pete. The final verse can be recited by the whole class.

Question Time

Twenty-one children can ask the questions (addressed to a visiting author), each one shooting a hand up (or in a smaller group, the questions can simply be shared out). The final question can be asked by the whole class.

Queue for the Zoo

Children can form a queue to perform this poem. As well as reciting the words they can mime the animal actions and make their sounds.

The Rhythm of Life
The children can be divided into seven groups. Each group can recite a couplet, with appropriate hand actions. Then the whole class can recite the final eight lines together.

Rum Tum Tugger
The chorus can be chanted by the whole class, with the other lines allocated to about twenty individuals.

Soldier, Soldier, Won't You Marry Me?
At our school, the boys lined up on one side of the room, the girls on the other. The boys chanted the soldier's lines while marching towards the girls, and then marched backwards while the girls marched towards them, chanting the maid's lines – and so on, back and forth. Or you could choose a girl and boy to mime the action while the rest of the class say the lines, again divided between girls and boys.

The Sound Collector
The whole class recites the first and last verses, with the other sound examples being divided between sixteen individuals or pairs.

Spells
For the first ten verses, an individual can speak the first line while the whole class chants the second line. This pattern is reversed in the final verse.

Sshhhhhh!
Three different children can speak a verse each, with everyone joining in all the shhh sounds. The final "Shhhhhhhh" should be a long one, fading out to nothing.

Tea with Aunty Mabel
Each instruction can be spoken by a different voice, with the whole class performing the last two lines.

There Was an Old Lady
The children can be divided into seven groups
(fly, spider, bird, cat, dog, cow, horse). Rather than
taking a whole verse, each group speaks the lines
relating to their animal (for instance, the spider
group always says, "She swallowed the spider to catch
the fly."). The whole class can say the repeated line,
"Perhaps she'll die." and the final line, "She's dead
of course."

This is the Key to the Castle
The first line can be spoken in chorus. Then different
groups can recite the verses, with a single child
speaking the final verse.

The Three-Headed Dog
Three children are needed for this. Their bodies could
be covered with a single brown sheet or blanket, from
which the three heads emerge.

To Every Thing There Is a Season
This can be performed by fifteen children (or pairs of
children) each reading two lines. Or the lines could be
shared out among a smaller group.

Today, I Feel
The whole class recites the first and the last lines, and
the other lines can be spoken by individual children.

Trading
Divide up the lines, with the whole class shouting "So I
quit" at the end. Some props or miming could turn this
into more of a performance.

The Treasures
The whole class can ask the questions, and eleven
children can voice the Barn Owl, Tiger, Peacock etc

who give the answers. This could work well with simple costumes, or artwork, perhaps carried aloft on sticks.

The Tree and the Pool
The whole class can recite the first three lines of the third verse, while the other lines are divided between individuals.

The Trouble with My Brother
The whole class chants the chorus, and the verses are divided up between individuals or groups.

Twenty-Four Hours
This can be divided into twenty-four voices, one for each hour of the day. Any remaining children, or else the whole class, can recite the first four and the last four lines.

The Visitor
Individuals can act the man, the wife and the skeleton, with the narration being spoken by the whole class or else divided up among them.

Voices of Water
Individual children (or pairs) can recite each line, and the whole class can say the last line together.

What a Shame You Lost Your Tail
The children can be divided into seven individual animals for the first seven verses and two groups of humans for the last two verses.

What I Love About School
This poem can either be divided into twelve verses, each recited by a different child, or it could be performed by just two children, one voicing the "What I love" verses and the other the "What I hate" verses.

Where Are You Going, Johnny?
One child can act Johnny, with the remaining lines either being spoken by the whole class, by one child, or by different individuals.

Witch, Witch
Either two children can perform this (one acting the witch and the other asking the questions), or else a class can ask the questions with one child replying.

Worm Words
Just two voices are required for this one. It might be fun to make a worm puppet with two hand-holes.

The Wraggle Taggle Gipsies
With two children acting the lord and the lady, and the rest of the children put into two groups, the poem can be divided up as follows:
Group 1: Verses 1, 3
Group 2: Verses 2, 5
Lord: Verses 4, 6, 8
Lady: Verse 7, 9 (or the whole class could chant the last line)

Yellow Butter
This tongue-twister can be recited by four groups (each starting off "Yellow butter"), with "Don't talk with your mouth full" being spoken by a single child, or else by the first three groups.

You Can't Stop Me!
The whole class can chant the refrain "Not now, not ever . . . never" and the rest of the text can be divided up between individuals or groups. It might be effective for more voices to be joining for each section, as the water grows, so the volume increases until the whole class is chanting the final "Not now, not ever . . . never!" And then a single voice comes in as the Sea for the final couplet.

Index of Poets

Index of Titles and First Lines

Titles are in *italics*. Where the title and first line are the same, the first line only is listed.

Acknowledgements

JOHN AGARD, 'What a Shame You Lost Your Tail' copyright © John Agard 1996 and 'Don't Call Alligator Long-Mouth Till You Cross the River' copyright © John Agard 1986, reproduced by kind permission of John Agard c/o Caroline Sheldon Literary Agency Limited;

ALLAN AHLBERG, 'Blame' from *Please Mrs Butler* by Allan Ahlberg (Kestrel 1983, Puffin Books 1984) copyright © Allan Ahlberg 1983, reproduced by permission of Penguin Books Ltd;

W. H. AUDEN, 'O What is that Sound' copyright © W. H. Auden 1936, renewed; reprinted by permission of Curtis Brown Ltd;

JAMES BERRY, 'People Equal' from *A Nest Full of Stars* by James Berry, Macmillan Children's Books (2002) copyright © James Berry 2002, by permission of the author;

CLARE BEVAN, 'The Blind Dog' from *Taking My Human for a Walk*, ed. Roger Stevens (2003) Macmillan Children's Books, 'The Three-Headed Dog' from *Read Me Out Loud*, ed. Tokzec and Cookson (2007) Macmillan Children's Books, 'The Treasures' and 'Queue for the Zoo' copyright © Clare Bevan 2012, all by permission of the author;

DAVE CALDER, 'This is the Key to the Castle' copyright © Dave Calder 1987, first published in *Bamboozled* (1987) Other, by permission of the author;

JAMES CARTER, 'Pirate Pete' from *Hey, Little Bug! Poems for Little Creatures* by James Carter (2011) Frances Lincoln, by permission of the author;

CHARLES CAUSLEY, 'Twenty-Four Hours' from *Collected Poems for Children*, Macmillan Children's Books, by permission of David Higham Associates on behalf of the author;

JUNE CREBBIN, 'Dinner-Time Rhyme' from *The Jungle Sale* (1988) Viking, by permission of the author;

JULIA DONALDSON, 'Nut Tree' (2004), 'Chess' (2013), 'Question Time' (2004), 'Hands' (2004), 'I've Got a Ball of Pastry' (2011), 'The Food Train' (2004) and 'Sshhhhhh!' (2004) all copyright © Julia Donaldson,